Getting To Know...

Nature's Children

ELK

Pamela Martin

PUBLISHER	Joseph R. DeVarennes	
PUBLICATION DIRECTOR	Kenneth H. Pearson	
MANAGING EDITOR	Valerie Wyatt	
SERIES ADVISOR	Merebeth Switzer	
SERIES CONSULTANT	Michael Singleton	
CONSULTANTS	Ross James	
	Kay McKeever	
	Dr. Audrey N. Tomera	
ADVISORS	Roger Aubin	
	Robert Furlonger	
	Gaston Lavoie	
EDITORIAL SUPERVISOR	Jocelyn Smyth	
PRODUCTION MANAGER	Ernest Homewood	
PRODUCTION ASSISTANTS	Penelope Moir	
	Brock Piper	
EDITORS	Katherine Farris	Anne Minguet-Patocka
	Sandra Gulland	Sarah Reid
	Cristel Kleitsch	Cathy Ripley
	Elizabeth MacLeod	Eleanor Tourtel
	Pamela Martin	Karin Velcheff
PHOTO EDITORS	Bill Ivy	
	Don Markle	
DESIGN	Annette Tatchell	
CARTOGRAPHER	Jane Davie	
PUBLICATION ADMINISTRATION	Kathy Kishimoto	
	Monique Lemonnier	
ARTISTS	Marianne Collins	Greg Ruhl
	Pat Ivy	Mary Theberge

This series is approved and recommended by the Federation of Ontario Naturalists.

JD BM

Canadian Cataloguing in Publication Data

Martin, Pamela.
  Elks

(Getting to know—nature's children)
Includes index.
ISBN 0-7172-1940-2

1. Elk—Juvenile literature.
I. Title. II. Series.

QL737.U55M37 1985   j599.73'57   C85-098712-1

Have you ever wondered . . .

933407

Think of a huge sack of potatoes. Now imagine carrying it on your head. Most people would have trouble lifting a huge sack of potatoes in their arms, let alone carrying it on their heads. But if you *did* manage it, you would probably have a tough time holding your head up.

Believe it or not, an adult male elk, or wapiti, as it is sometimes called, carries antlers that may weigh 18 to 23 kilograms (40-50 pounds). Instead of being bowed down by the weight, the elk carries its head high, almost as if it is showing off its handsome antlers.

With its regal crown of antlers and its majestic bearing, it is no wonder that the elk is sometimes called the "monarch of the mountain."

A Cool Dip

Like you, elk enjoy nothing better than a cool dip in a lake on a hot summer day. But just when a group of elk mothers have found a nice place for a swim, a group of young elk calves comes splashing past. Water sprays everywhere. The mothers do not seem to mind, though. They watch calmly as the calves chase each other along the shoreline.

With its long legs, an elk calf loves to run. All this exercise helps the calf's muscles grow strong. That is important for a young elk. When it is only about six months old it must travel with the herd to the winter feeding grounds.

Elk are strong and graceful. Their usual pace is an unhurried walk, but they can run quite fast when necessary.

Deer Cousins

Elk are members of the deer family. They are cousins to the White-tailed Deer, caribou and moose.

Like most families, the deer family has certain things in common. All its members have split hoofs, and none of them has any top front teeth. Like cows they quickly swallow their food and later bring lumps back into their mouths to chew.

You can probably think of some other animals who share these characteristics. But there is one way in which the members of the deer family are unique. All the males grow and shed a set of antlers every year.

The elk must take care; at this stage of their growth antlers are very soft and can easily be damaged.

A Deer of Different Names

The elk has been given different names by different peoples. The Shawnee, one of the native peoples of North America, called it "wapiti," which means white rump. Even though the elk's rump patch is more tan colored than white, you can see where this name came from.

When English people first settled in North America, they called this great deer "elk" because it looked a little like the elk they had known in Europe. That elk, however, is the animal North Americans call a moose. Confusing, isn't it?

Today the North American elk is known by either name—elk or wapiti.

Heavy headgear.

10

How Big is Big?

Elk are big. Of all their close North American relatives, only the moose is bigger. The male elk, or stag, can grow to be two and a half metres (8 feet) long from nose to tail and weigh anywhere from 265 to 500 kilograms (580-1120 pounds).

But elk are not tall animals. At their shoulder, they are only about 140 centimetres (55 inches) tall. Female elk, or hinds, are smaller than stags.

Where elk live in North America.

Different Coats for Different Seasons

The elk has a beautiful and useful coat. It changes with the seasons to help the elk keep warm or cool.

In the summer, the elk's coat is a single layer of short, stiff, glossy hair. Its face, neck, belly and legs are dark brown. Its tail and the heart-shaped patch on its rump are light brown or beige.

This light coat is perfect for hot summer weather, but the elk needs something warmer for winter. So, as summer draws to a close, it gradually sheds its short summer hair and grows a thick new coat. This is called molting.

Winter Woollies

By the end of September, the elk's old coat is completely gone and a new grayish brown one has grown in.

The elk's winter coat has two layers: a short, woolly undercoat and, on top, a layer of long, coarse guard hairs. On the elk's sides and belly, these guard hairs are about as long as your finger. On its neck and shoulders, they are about as long as your hand. They grow so long across the front of its neck that they make a mane.

The extra thickness of the elk's winter coat makes it look more solid and less graceful than it does in the summer—just as you look chunkier in your winter clothes than you do in your summer T-shirt and shorts.

When spring comes again, the elk no longer needs its winter protection. Its heavy coat is ragged and worn. It falls out in tufts while its summer coat grows in underneath. By June, the winter coat is all gone and the elk looks sleek and fresh again with its short summer hair.

Opposite page:

It's easy to tell that these are elk. Unlike deer, both the mother and calf have a dark brown mane.

A Rack of Antlers

Coats are not the only things elk shed. Male elk (and, very occasionally, females) grow and shed their antlers each year too.

In February, the place where the antlers are attached begins to weaken. Often one antler will fall off before the other, and so the elk may spend weeks with its head weighed down on one side. When an antler falls off, it makes a sharp cracking sound.

After an elk's old antlers fall off, it is left with two bony stumps on its head. Almost immediately, the tips of the stumps begin to swell and new antlers begin to sprout. They are covered by soft skin called velvet. Blood flows through the velvet and brings food to the soft, growing antlers. By midsummer, the antlers will be fully grown and will have hardened into strong bone.

Warm winter wear.

Ragged Headgear

When the elk's antlers are fully grown, the velvet is no longer needed. It dries up and begins to itch. The elk helps strip it off by rubbing its antlers against bushes and shrubs. The rubbing soon leaves the new antlers bare and shiny, and plant juices darken them from white to rich brown.

Elk keep their antlers all through the fall and winter. Male elk need them to challenge and fight other stags in the mating season.

By late summer the velvet hangs in strips from the elk's antlers.

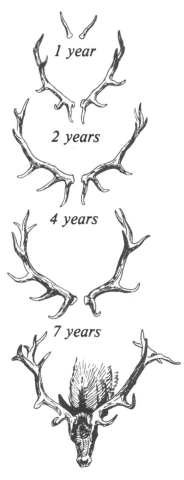

1 year

2 years

4 years

7 years

8 years

Reading Antlers

An elk's antlers can help tell you how old it is and whether or not it is healthy. Here is how to "read" antlers to find out about their owner.

If the antlers are simple long, thin spikes, the elk is probably one year old. By age two, an elk's antlers are thicker and have three or four points each. By the time an elk is four, the antlers will have six points each.

After that, elk usually do not grow any more antler points. But the antlers do get heavier each year until age seven or eight. By then, they curve back over the elk's body.

A full-grown male's antlers may be more than one and a half metres (5 feet) long. And they will be heavy—about as heavy as a child of four or five. When a stag gets old or sick, his antlers grow in thinner, with fewer points and sometimes in odd shapes.

Stags use their antlers mainly to fight for mates. The fights are seldom very serious as one stag will usually give up before any real damage is done.

Getting Around

Elk are well-equipped for moving. They have long, powerful legs and hard, black hoofs that allow them to walk easily and safely over rough ground.

Elk usually walk slowly, but if they want to avoid danger, they can gallop at speeds of up to about 48 kilometres (30 miles) an hour for short distances. That is about as fast as cars go on city streets.

With such strong legs, elk are very good jumpers. An elk was once seen jumping a fence that was higher than a tall man.

Elk track

Elk hoof

Dusk or dawn is the best time to spot an elk.

Elk Days

Elk are most active in the morning and early evening. This is when they eat. They spend the middle of the day resting and chewing their food.

In good weather, they also spend a lot of time scratching and grooming to clean the bugs and dirt from their coats. They lick and chew as much of their coats as they can reach. They even use their hind legs to scratch their necks and heads.

At night elk usually rest close to their feeding grounds. They often choose high places from which they can see or smell danger. Elk do not have a bed like you do or even a special place to sleep. They just lie down in the nearest comfortable spot. They take short snoozes rather than all-night sleeps. And while most of the elk are sleeping, one always stays awake to watch for danger.

Rain and cold do not bother elk much, but on really windy days they may take shelter among trees or bushes.

Opposite page:

Elk will not hesitate to enter the water as they are excellent swimmers.

What is Home to an Elk?

Elk used to live all across central and northern North America. But as people built farms and towns on much of the land, the elk moved to places that were still wild.

Elk need two sorts of country side by side: open areas for feeding and trees or bush for finding shelter and safety. Today these are harder to find. Now most elk live in the wilds of the western mountains, moving to higher or lower ground according to the seasons.

They spend the summers high up in the mountain meadows. But winters are hard there. Deep snow covers the ground and makes it hard to find food and even to move around. Because of this the elk would be easy prey for cougars, wolves and other hungry hunters.

So, as winter deepens, the elk travel slowly down the mountains to more sheltered valleys. In the spring, as the snow melts, they journey back up the mountain to their summer grounds.

Grazing in the sun.

Food for an Elk

Elk are big animals and they have appetites to match. They need to eat almost 10 kilograms (22 pounds) of food a day. Their diet changes with the seasons, and so does the amount of time they spend feeding. It can take a lot longer in winter to find enough food to satisfy an elk-size appetite.

In summer, elk eat grasses, weeds, wild flowers, clover and even mushrooms. In winter, most elk will eat whatever grasses they can find, using their hoofs to dig through the snow covering. Whenever possible, they graze on hillsides where the wind has blown away much of the snow. They also eat the tender twigs they find on trees and bushes.

If food becomes very scarce in winter, elk will even eat the bark of trees and fir or pine needles.

In the winter, elk band together in sheltered valleys where the snow is not too deep.

Ready to Eat

The elk's body is specially suited to its diet of grasses and twigs. It has sharp front bottom teeth and a hard pad on the top of its mouth. It scrapes its teeth against this pad to tear off mouthfuls of food.

When an elk eats, it does not chew its food thoroughly the way you do. Instead, it swallows food quickly and stores it in a special part of its stomach.

When it has eaten enough, it moves to a sheltered place and brings the stored food, or cud, back to its mouth for chewing.

This swallow-now-chew-later arrangement means the elk can graze quickly. It does not have to stay out in the open for long, where enemies might spot it. It can chew in peace later, safely out of sight of hungry eyes.

Slim pickings!

Family Life

You probably live with the same people—your family—month in and month out. But elk group together in different ways at different times of the year.

In summer, hinds and their young live in a small herd of 10 to 25 animals. When fall mating season begins, a stag joins the herd. He fights off other stags who want to take his place, mates with the hinds in his herd and keeps them from wandering away.

As the weather turns colder, the elk begin the journey to their winter grounds. The small herds band together into larger ones. About 100 elk of different ages and both sexes will spend the winter together. After all their fall fighting and herding, the stags are too worn out to lead this large herd. Instead a hind, who is strong after an autumn of grazing, becomes the leader.

In spring, the stags leave the large herd to spend the summer in small bands. The bands have no leader, and the stags come and go as they please.

Opposite page:

There's no shortage of food here.

Elk Talk

Elk are probably the noisiest members of the deer family. If you could eavesdrop on a large herd of elk, you would hear a strange combination of snorts, bugles and squeals.

Elk make a snorting sound, called a bark, when they are frightened or alarmed. At mating time, male elk "bugle" to one another. This bugling sound may be the male elk's way of challenging other males to a fight over a female.

Young elk squeal when frightened or hungry. They seem to change the loudness and pitch of their squeal depending on what it is that is wrong. Although humans may have trouble figuring out what these squeals mean, the mother elk always seems to know just what to do for her youngster.

Some elk herds are surprisingly stable. Occasionally a hind will spend her life with the same herd her mother belonged to.

Freckled Babies

In late May or early June, it is time for the mother elk to give birth. They do not dig dens or build nurseries for their young. Instead, they simply leave the herd and search for a safe place hidden from predators.

Usually only one calf is born, but sometimes there are twins.

Elk calves are big. Newborns weigh about 17 kilograms (37 pounds). That is as much as five or six human babies! They are reddish brown and freckled with off-white spots that run in rows down their back and sides.

The Roosevelt or Olympic Elk is the largest wapiti in North America.

Long Legs

A baby elk can stand when it is only an hour or two old, but it is very shaky on its long, skinny legs. Every time its mother licks it, it is in danger of toppling over.

At first the calf's only food is its mother's milk. It gets strong quickly on this rich diet. In a few days it can follow its mother around, and within a week it can run easily.

Soon it will begin to nibble on grasses and leaves just as its mother does. But it will not stop nursing until early fall.

Mother and calf emerge from the morning mist.

Danger!

The most dangerous time of an elk's life is when it is very young. This is when it is easiest prey for its natural enemies—cougars, golden eagles, bobcats, wolves, coyotes or bears. While an adult elk can often protect itself from predators with a kick of its hoofs, or escape by running away, a very young calf cannot.

But an elk mother is very protective of her baby. Until the calf is strong enough to join a summer herd, she always feeds within earshot. If it squeals in fright, she runs back to defend it. And if she senses danger, she barks a warning. Instantly, the calf drops to the ground and stays very still. Its spotted coat blends into its surroundings making it almost invisible. And since its scent is very faint, predators cannot usually sniff it out.

Joining the Herd

When the calf is strong enough to travel, mother and baby join a small group of other hinds and their young. Soon the elk calves are frisking and frolicking together. They run around and play chase games, splash about in the water, playfight and sometimes even toss sticks.

While some mothers feed or rest, other hinds "calf sit." They keep an eye on the lively youngsters and watch for danger.

Young calf on the alert.

Growing Up

A calf stays with its mother through its first winter and often into the following spring. But with the spring comes a new calf. When it is born, the hind drives last year's calf away.

The yearling is now an independent member of the herd. But even though it is on its own, it will not be an adult for several more years. A young hind will not bear her first calf until she is three years old. A young stag will not mate until he is four or five.

By then, the young elk will have grown to be elegant, stately animals who may live to be fifteen years old and produce several calves of their own.

Special Words

Antlers Hard, bony growths on the head of male elk.

Calf A young elk.

Cud Hastily swallowed food brought back for chewing by animals such as elk and deer.

Guard hairs Long coarse hairs that make up the outer layer of the elk's winter coat.

Hind A female elk.

Hoofs Feet of elk, deer, cattle and some other animals.

Mate To come together to produce young.

Mating season The time of the year during which animals mate.

Migrate To make regular journeys every year in search of food.

Molt To shed one coat and grow another.

Points Tips of antlers.

Predator An animal that hunts other animals for food.

Prey An animal hunted by another animal for food.

Rack Set of antlers.

Stag A male elk.

Velvet Soft skin which covers antlers as they grow.

Yearling An animal that is a year old.

INDEX

Cover Photo: Wayne Lankinen (Valan Photos)

Photo Credits: Dennis Schmidt (Valan Photos), pages 4, 24, 43; J.D. Markou (Valan Photos), pages 7, 12, 16, 35; Stephen J. Krasemann (Valan Photos), pages 8, 36; Robert J. Rose (Miller Services), page 11; Wayne Lankinen (Valan Photos) pages 15, 20, 23, 27, 28; J.D. Markou (Miller Services), page 19; Esther Schmidt, page 31; Kennon Cooke (Valan Photos), page 32; Thomas Kitchin (Valan Photos), pages 39, 44; J.D. Taylor (Miller Services), page 43.

Getting To Know...

Nature's Children

MICE

Susan Horner
and
Celia B. Lottridge

PUBLISHER	Joseph R. DeVarennes
PUBLICATION DIRECTOR	Kenneth H. Pearson
MANAGING EDITOR	Valerie Wyatt
SERIES ADVISOR	Merebeth Switzer
SERIES CONSULTANT	Michael Singleton
CONSULTANTS	Ross James
	Kay McKeever
	Dr. Audrey N. Tomera
ADVISORS	Roger Aubin
	Robert Furlonger
	Gaston Lavoie
EDITORIAL SUPERVISOR	Jocelyn Smyth
PRODUCTION MANAGER	Ernest Homewood
PRODUCTION ASSISTANTS	Penelope Moir
	Brock Piper

EDITORS

Katherine Farris   Anne Minguet-Patocka
Sandra Gulland   Sarah Reid
Cristel Kleitsch   Cathy Ripley
Elizabeth MacLeod   Eleanor Tourtel
Pamela Martin   Karin Velcheff

PHOTO EDITORS	Bill Ivy
	Don Markle
DESIGN	Annette Tatchell
CARTOGRAPHER	Jane Davie
PUBLICATION ADMINISTRATION	Kathy Kishimoto
	Monique Lemonnier

ARTISTS

Marianne Collins   Greg Ruhl
Pat Ivy   Mary Theberge

This series is approved and recommended by the Federation of Ontario Naturalists.

Canadian Cataloguing in Publication Data

Horner, Susan
  Mice

(Getting to know—nature's children)
Includes index.
ISBN 0-7172-1903-8

1. Mice—Juvenile literature.
I. Lottridge, Celia. II. Title. III. Series.

QL737.R638H67 1985   j599.32'33   C85-098721-0

Have you ever wondered . . .

Mice probably turn up in more stories, nursery rhymes, fables and cartoons than any other animal. But do all these make-believe mice tell us very much about real mice?

Think for a moment of Aesop's fable about the Town Mouse and the Country Mouse. The Town Mouse invites the Country Mouse to visit him, boasting of his splendid house and the exciting things to do—and eat—in the city. At first the Country Mouse is very impressed by everything, especially by all the fancy city food. But he soon learns that city life can be noisy and dangerous too. Before long the Country Mouse packs up and heads back to his own home where he lives simply but in peace.

Have you ever wondered just what sort of life the Country Mouse was going back to? What sort of house did it have? What did it eat? And was life in the country really less exciting—and less dangerous—than life in the city? Let's take a closer look at some "country mice" to find out.

Opposite page:

The long whiskers of the White-footed Mouse are very sensitive and enable it to feel objects in the dark.

Mice Everywhere

In the real world, as in story books, mice are everywhere.

Forest, field, mountain, brushland, hot or cold, wet or dry—nearly every kind of landscape and climate is home to one or more kinds of mice. There are mice that live in the far north and spend much of their lives in tunnels under the snow, and there are mice that spend their days in ground burrows avoiding the hot sun of their desert homes. There are mice that live in marshy places and are excellent swimmers, and mice that nest in trees and may spend their whole life without ever touching the ground.

The Northern Red-backed Vole lives in northern Canada and Alaska.

In North America alone there are hundreds of kinds of mice. Some live only in one tiny area. The Sitka Mouse, for instance, is found only on the smaller Queen Charlotte Islands off Canada's west coast. Other kinds of mice are found almost all across the continent.

If Aesop had been writing his story in North America, his Country Mouse would probably have been a Deer Mouse or a Meadow Vole.

Deer Mice are the most widespread of all North American mice. They live about as far north as the tree line and all the way south through Central Mexico. About the only place you will not find Deer Mice is in Florida or other swampy regions of the South. They prefer reasonably dry country.

Meadow Voles are almost as widespread as Deer Mice, but they are a little fussier about the kind of country they live in. They quite like fairly wet regions but avoid dense forests and dry grasslands.

Opposite page:

The Deer Mouse is sometimes called "wood mouse," since it often lives in the forest.

Mouse

Vole

A Mouse by Any Other Name

Mice are rodents. They are distant relatives of beavers, muskrats, porcupines, squirrels and chipmunks and cousins of lemmings and rats. The main thing all rodents have in common is very sharp front teeth that never stop growing.

The mouse's closest cousins are the voles. You have probably seen a vole, even though you may not have known it by its correct name. The most widespread vole of all, the Meadow Vole, is the little scampering creature often seen in barns, farmyards and fields. It is commonly called the field mouse.

It is not surprising that people mix up mice and voles; they are very much alike. So how can we tell who is who? Generally speaking, mice are more slender than voles, their faces are more pointed, their ears and eyes bigger and their tails longer.

The Meadow Vole is probably the most familiar rodent in North America.

How to Meet a Mouse

Walk through any field or woods and you probably pass very near any number of mice and voles without even knowing it. To actually meet a mouse, you must choose your time carefully. Most mice and voles are active mainly from dusk to dawn. Then you will have to be very patient and alert.

Patient because you will have to sit very still. Mice are timid creatures, ready to flee at any hint of danger. In most cases, their eyesight is not very good, but they have a keen sense of hearing. The slightest sound you might make—a sniff or a cracking twig or a rustle of leaves—will send them scurrying for cover. With strong legs to help it run fast and jump far, a frightened mouse will be gone before you can catch a glimpse of it.

Peek-a-boo!

Now You See It, Now You Don't

You must also be alert to get a good look at a mouse. Why? Mice come in a variety of shades and combinations of grays and browns. These colors blend in well with their surroundings and make them difficult to see.

Deer Mice get their name from their coloring, which resembles that of a deer—reddish brown with lighter underparts. But over time, even Deer Mice have developed variations. Those that live in shadowy woodlands are darker than those that live in the open.

You can tell by the color of this Deer Mouse's coat that its home is in the woods.

Small as a Mouse

We all know that mice are small. But there is small . . . and there is small. The tiniest full-grown North American mouse may be only 12 centimetres (5 inches) long, and about half of that is tail! A mouse that size may weigh as little as 11 grams (less than half an ounce). The largest mice are about twice that size.

Even within one kind of mouse there can be great variations. Deer Mice, for instance, come in a wide range of sizes. Once again, the largest is about twice as big as the smallest.

It's no mystery how the Red-backed Vole got its name.

Tails That Tell Tales

It is generally true that voles have shorter tails than true mice, but just as with overall size there is a great deal of variation. The Meadow Vole's tail is only about one-third the length of the rest of its body, while the Long-tailed Vole's tail is more than half as long as its body.

And there can be surprisingly big differences within one group. Some kinds of Deer Mice have tails that are only about half as long as their body, while others have tails that are longer than their body. The length of a Deer Mouse's tail can tell you something about how and where it lives. Those with longer tails usually do a lot of tree climbing. They use their longer tails for balance. Shorter-tailed Deer Mice usually live where there are few or no trees.

Tiny acrobat!

Mice in Motion

Scurry, scamper, scuttle . . . these are the words we associate with mice on the move. In fact, mice always seem to be in a hurry, dashing here and there and back again on their little, sharply clawed feet.

Many mice are also good climbers, and some are excellent swimmers. A few can even swim across streams. Some mice take to water mainly to escape predators, but others seem to dive in just for the fun of it.

And most mice can jump. In fact one family of mice can jump so well that they are called—what else—Jumping Mice. These mice have extra long hind feet, and the best jumpers among them can leap as far as three to four metres (yards). That is about 16 times the length of their body from their twitchy little nose to the tip of their long tail. Very few human long jumpers can come close to jumping even five times their own height.

Woodland Jumping Mouse.

Jumping Mouse paw prints

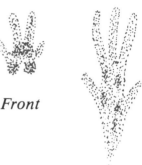

Front

Hind

White-footed Mouse paw prints

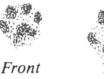

Front

Hind

Homebodies

Aesop's Country Mouse did not seem to mind traveling from his country home to the city. But most mice are not great travelers. Many spend their entire lives dashing to and fro in an area that is probably not much bigger than your back yard. The few kinds that do wander farther afield rarely go more than the length of a city block in any direction from their nest. The area a mouse regularly travels is known as its home range, and the mouse knows every nook, cranny, dip and bump in it.

While few mice ever leave their home range, they do not usually mind sharing it. When their babies are small—and in some cases even at other times—they are very defensive of the area right around their nest. But home ranges will usually overlap without anyone getting upset.

The Meadow Vole tends to be active both day and night, stopping every now and then to take short naps.

Mouse Trails

You would think that mice must have a hard time getting around in woods and fields. After all, their little legs may be very strong but they are also very short. The loose layer of fallen leaves and pine needles that usually covers the forest floor would be thigh-deep to most mice, and meadow grasses would loom as tall as giant oaks would to you—with a lot less space in between. So how do mice manage?

Have you ever noticed that if people use a shortcut across a lawn or through a field, the grass and plants soon stop growing there? Well, the same principle works for mice. They establish a network of tiny paths, sometimes even with bridges and tunnels, that go from their nests to various useful spots.

Some may be able to beat a path down just by their repeated comings and goings. Others bite off the grasses in their way and then trample down the stubs. And some do not bother doing all this hard work themselves. They simply use highways or burrows built by their relatives.

Opposite page:

A Deer Mouse out on a limb!

Danger Everywhere

Mouse highways are not just a lazy mouse's way of making life a little easier for itself. It is very important that mice move as quickly as possible and that they have a fast easy way to dash back to their nest.

Why? Because mice have a great many enemies. These include foxes, coyotes, weasels, skunks, raccoons, bears, shrews, squirrels, a number of snakes, turtles, fish and birds of prey. The list changes a bit with the kind of mouse and its habits. For example, mice that are active at night do not have to worry about hawks or eagles. And those that seldom or never take to water have no fishy predators. But it is safe to say that any animal that eats meat sees a mouse as an appetizing dinner.

This may seem unfair to mice, but you must remember that it is all part of the balance of nature. If all mice lived to grow up and have babies, there would soon be so many there would be no plants. The mice would eat them all. On the other hand, if there were not so many mice, many animals would starve.

Opposite page:

On the alert.

Mouse Menus

For creatures who never go very far, mice certainly do a great deal of running around. You can probably guess what they are doing: they are searching for food. Like many wild animals, mice spend most of their waking hours finding food and eating it.

In general mice are not fussy eaters. They will eat whatever is available, and they will eat a lot of it. This does not mean that different kinds of mice do not have their favorite foods. Deer Mice prefer seeds, but they will also nibble at buds and tender green leaves in the spring. Meadow Voles are mainly grass eaters, but they will make do with seeds, roots and even twig bark when grass runs out.

Almost all mice seem to enjoy an occasional tasty meat snack such as a caterpillar, cutworm or spider. And one mouse, the Northern Grasshopper Mouse, eats mainly insects. Although it will eat amost any kind of insect or insect egg, its very favorite is—you guessed it—grasshoppers.

Opposite page:

Some Mice will go to great lengths for a meal.

Clean and Tidy

Would it surprise you to hear that mice and cats have something in common? Actually, it is something they share with many animals— they like to keep clean.

A mouse sits up on its haunches to groom itself, using its tail for extra support. It washes its face with its forepaws, carefully rubbing its ears. Then it strokes down its back, and belly, combing the fur with its tiny claws. Finally it uses its teeth and tongue to groom its feet and tail.

Mice also like to live in clean homes, and many establish special toilet areas away from their nest. Many mice live in colonies and those that do often set up community toilets, sharing the work of building the runways that lead to them.

Some mice, such as Deer Mice, do not bother building toilets. They seem to find it easier to build a new nest when the old one gets too dirty.

Opposite page:

The long tail of the Meadow Jumping Mouse helps this champion jumper balance itself as it hops.

30

Mouse Houses

Adult mice usually each have their own home nest, at least for most of the year. This is true of mice that live in colonies too.

Mouse houses come in many sizes. Most are ball shaped and made of grasses and twigs and anything else that is handy: bits of bone, cloth, fur, string, paper—whatever odds and ends the builder happens to find. The inside is hollow and lined with softer material such as dandelions or thistle down, moss or cattails.

Mice build their nests almost anywhere that is protected enough for the owner to feel safe. Some mice hide their nests in underground burrows they dig themselves, while some borrow burrows abandoned by other animals. Other favorite hiding places are under logs and rocks, in tree hollows or stumps, in clumps of grass or weeds. Mice have even been known to take over deserted birds' nests.

This Deer Mouse has taken up residence in a hollow log.

This is how a Jumping Mouse hibernates. Its tail is curled up around its body.

Opposite page:

The House Mouse is not native to North America. Its ancestors came over on ships with the settlers.

Mice in Winter

Much like people, mice have various ways of coping with the cold and snow of winter.

Jumping Mice hibernate. They put on a layer of fat in the fall and go into a deep sleep until spring. The extra fat provides what little energy their body needs.

Most mice and voles, however, remain active all winter—though some more so than others. Many kinds of mice have stretchy cheek pouches in which they collect seeds. In the autumn they start gathering as many as they can and hide them in storage chambers near the nest. As long as their store lasts, they only have to make very short trips to their food caches.

These mice spend the rest of the time huddled up together in groups of 10 to 15 for warmth. Among White-footed Mice, there is a definite "pecking order" in the group. One mouse quickly establishes itself as top mouse and gets the warmest spot in the middle. The least aggressive members of the group end up on the colder edges.

Business as Usual

Most voles do not collect very much extra food in the fall. They are, therefore, almost as active during the winter as they are in summer.

Those that live mainly underground travel back and forth through their tunnels as usual. Meadow Voles and others tunnel through the snow to use the same surface runways they use in summer.

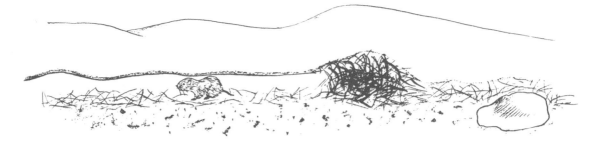

Mice use tunnels under the snow to get around during the winter.

All voles must eat their own weight in food each day to survive.

Squeal, Chatter, Cheep

You would not find it easy to eavesdrop on a mouse "conversation." Some mice hardly ever make sounds, and even the more talkative ones have very soft, small voices.

Those soft voices, however, can make a surprising variety of sounds. Most mice squeak and squeal, and many chirp and chatter as well. A few whistle in a way that sounds rather like an insect's hum. The Singing Vole is even named for its high-pitched, throbbing call. And, believe it or not, the Grasshopper Mouse sometimes sits on its haunches, throws back its head and howls like a miniature coyote!

Some mice have special sounds they make for certain occasions. For instance, many thump when alarmed— some with their front paws, others with their tail. And some female mice have a special squeak that lets males know they are ready to mate.

The Singing Vole—minstrel of the tundra!

Starting a Family

When mice are ready to mate—several times a year—the male and female share a nest for a few days. They will spend these days courting; they groom each other and chase each other around the area near the nest.

Depending on the kind of mouse, the male may leave after mating or he may stay nearby and help care for the babies after they are born. Either way, the mother prepares the nursery by herself. She either relines her nest with the softest material she can find or builds a brand new one.

These newborn Deer Mice are feeding on their mother's milk.

Big Families

The babies are born about three weeks after the parents mate. There are usually five to seven babies in a litter but sometimes many more. The number depends on the kind of mouse and often on the age of the mother and how well she has been eating.

Newborn mice are tiny—less than four centimetres (1.5 inches) long including their tails. That is shorter than most erasers! They are blind, deaf and have no hair except for tiny whiskers.

Fast-Growing Babies

Baby mice grow amazingly fast. For the first two days their mother does not leave the nest, and the babies nurse almost continually. Their skin is so transparent that you would actually be able to see the milk flowing into them.

A family of White-footed Mice.

Within four days, however, the babies have a little fur. In one week they have doubled their birth weight. In two weeks they can see and are moving around. They are still nursing but they can also eat berries and seeds.

Mice are careful mothers, especially Deer Mice. If the nest is disturbed a Deer Mouse mother will take her babies to a safer place. They stay with her by holding on tight to a nipple. If a baby should fall off, the mother will pick it up in her mouth by the scruff of the neck and carry it to the new nest.

If the father is still around, he helps keep the babies warm by cuddling up to them and helps keep them clean. He also repairs the nest and will go after any baby that strays and bring it home. Once the babies are old enough, he will take them on food-finding expeditions.

Out on his own!

Mice Forever

By the time they are a few weeks old, most mice are grown up and ready to fend for themselves. And by the time they are three or four months old, they are ready to start their own families. About the longest any can expect to live is about a year and a half. That may not seem like much, but it really is a lifetime to a mouse.

Few animals have learned to adapt to as many different conditions as mice, and few reproduce as rapidly. In spite of their short, hurried lives, you can be quite sure that next time you walk through a field or woods, somewhere very near some little mouse or vole is scampering about or snoozing in its nest.

So be sure you stop for a few minutes. Sit very still and watch carefully. And with a little bit of luck, your patience will be rewarded with a glimpse of the fascinating mini-world of mice.

Special Words

Burrow   A hole dug in the ground by an animal for use as a home.

Groom   Brush and clean hair or fur.

Hibernate   To go into a heavy sleep for the winter.

Home range   The area that a mouse regularly travels.

Litter   Young animals born together.

Mate   To come together to produce young.

Nurse   To drink the mother's milk.

Predator   An animal that hunts other animals for food.

Prey   An animal hunted by another animal for food. A bird that hunts animals for food is often called a bird of prey.

Rodent   An animal with teeth that are specially good for gnawing.

INDEX

Cover Photo: Bill Ivy

Photo Credits: Robert C. Simpson (Valan Photos), pages 4, 23, 43; J.R. Page (Valan Photos), pages 7, 39; Bill Ivy, pages 8, 11, 12, 15, 35, 36, 44; Duane Sept (Valan Photos), page 16; Michel Quintin (Valan Photos), pages 19, 24, 31; François Morneau (Valan Photos), page 20; Albert Kuhnigk (Valan Photos), page 27; Francis Lepine (Valan Photos), page 28; Dennis Schmidt (Valan Photos), page 32; John Fowler (Valan Photos), page 40.